NOVEL OUTLINING

STEP-BY-STEP

2 Manuscripts in 1 Book, Including:
How to Write a Novel and Outlining

Sandy Marsh

Table of Contents

BOOK 1: HOW TO WRITE A NOVEL 4
BOOK 2: OUTLINING 72

HOW TO WRITE A NOVEL

STEP-BY-STEP

ESSENTIAL ROMANCE NOVEL, MYSTERY NOVEL AND FANTASY NOVEL WRITING TRICKS ANY WRITER CAN LEARN

SANDY MARSH

BOOK 1: HOW TO WRITE A NOVEL

STEP-BY-STEP

Essential Romance Novel, Mystery Novel and Fantasy Novel Writing Tricks Any Writer Can Learn

Sandy Marsh

reparation, damages, or monetary loss due to the information herein, either directly or indirectly.

Respective authors own all copyrights not held by the publisher.

The information herein is offered for informational purposes solely, and is universal as so. The presentation of the information is without contract or any type of guarantee assurance.

The trademarks that are used are without any consent, and the publication of the trademark is without permission or backing by the trademark owner. All trademarks and brands within this book are for clarifying purposes only and are the owned by the owners themselves, not affiliated with this document.

Table of Contents

Introduction... **10**

Chapter 1: The Outline **12**

If You Love to Guide Your Focus… 13

If You Love Creative Freedom… 15

Questions to Ask Yourself........................... 18

Chapter 2: Your Setting **20**

If You Only Have One Location........................ 21

If You Have Many Locations 22

If You Are Making Up the Location 24

If You Only Have One Time Period........................ 26

If You Have Many Time Periods........................ 27

If You Are Making up the Time Period........................ 28

Combining the Two 29

Questions to Ask Yourself........................... 30

Chapter 3: The Point of View **33**

First Person 34

Second Person........................... 36

Third Person.. 37

Third Person Limited Omniscience 39

Third Person Unlimited Omniscience........................... 40

How to Choose.. 41

Questions to Ask Yourself.. 42

Chapter 4: Characters... **44**

The Value of Your Characters 45

Choosing Your Protagonist... 46

How Many Characters Do You Really Need?.............. 48

What Your Characters Say About Your Book.............. 49

Questions to Ask Yourself.. 50

Chapter 5: Conflict **52**

Types of Conflict 53

When the Conflict Should Occur.................................. 55

Questions to Ask Yourself.. 57

Chapter 6: Additional Tips **59**

Think Outside of the Box... 60

Ditch Expectations 62

Set Deadlines 63

Get a Good "Test" Reader 64

Avoid Perfectionism 65

Write What You Don't Know.. 66

Manipulate Your Reader's Emotions 67

Conclusion **69**

Introduction

Thank you and congratulations on purchasing *"How to Write a Novel: Step-by-Step | Essential Romance Novel, Mystery Novel and Fantasy Novel Writing Tricks Any Writer Can Learn"*. As well, congratulations on deciding that you want to write a fiction novel!

The tips and tricks you will learn in this book will help walk you through the step-by-step process of writing your very own novel, while also making it extremely easy to stay committed! You will learn everything you need to know about simplifying the process and making it one that you can easily stick to so that you can create the fiction novel of your dreams, literally!

Each chapter in this book is dedicated to one part of the novel writing experience. You will begin by learning all about outlines and work your way through each step right down to finding the perfect reader to test out your new novel. By the time you're done reading this you will be completely finished writing your very own fiction novel.

This book was designed to help make the process easier while also making it an enjoyable experience. Understand that this is not necessarily a "conventional" how-to book as it will seek to both educate and inform while also making the process fun and exciting. Writing a book should never be boring or difficult - if it is, you are going about it all wrong! With the steps in this book, you will learn to bring back the passion in your writing and create the best fiction novel possible, whether this is your first time trying or you've done this before and you just need a boost to get through this particular book!

Please be sure to take your time and have fun with this book as the writing process truly is an experience to be enjoyed. Allow each section to provide you with tips and tricks to help lighten up the experience so that you can increase the entertainment you derive from the writing process so that you are left not only with an incredible novel but also with an experience worth remembering. This book can be used as many times as you require, so be sure to keep it handy for any fiction novels you may set out to write! And lastly, please enjoy!

Chapter 1: The Outline

As you may be aware, having an outline to a book is important. This provides you with an idea of where the story is going and what your "goals" for the book are. Many authors prefer to start with a strong outline that will give them direction and help them stay on track when they are working through the writing process. Having a strong outline that identifies major plot points means that you can continually work your story towards each new plot point in chronological order so that you ultimately end up at your "goal" outcome based on what you had included in your outline.

For many writers, an outline is an absolute must-have. They prefer to have an outline that will help guide them because this keeps them focused and working along a credible storyline that is intended to keep readers engaged. By having this the writer knows how to stay on point and how to structure different parts of the story to keep everything working towards the same goal. For others, having an outline feels too boxy and they feel as though their creative expression is being suffocated by the existence of the outline. If this is you, then you may want to consider scratching the outline altogether. Below we will explore different tips and ideas for each unique individual and how you can create an incredible story regardless of whether or not you choose to use an outline.

If You Love to Guide Your Focus...

If you love to have your focus guided towards a particular goal, such as the one at the end of your outline, then having an outline is a good idea for you. This will help encourage you to stay on track with your writing process and keep each unique element of the story focused towards the outcome. Having the outline helps you avoid yourself from putting unnecessary information in the plot line or otherwise over-explaining things that may not be relevant to the overall story itself.

Outlines are a great tool to help keep writers focused and guided throughout the process. Creating an outline is fairly simple, you think of where you want the characters to "start" and "end" in the story. Then, you decide what major plot points are going to get them from the start to the end. For example, you might have two characters in a romance novel that are going to start as best friends and end as lovers. Along the way, you might choose to include plot points such as them taking on a big project together and it brings them closer, but the competitiveness between them drives them apart. As they work through the competitiveness they discover that their relationship grows even stronger and when they complete the project they are feeling closer than ever before. Later they make excuses to hang out even more, and eventually, they end up falling in love. As you can see from this example, the outline included the main characters, the starting and ending points of the story, and major events that lead the two characters to the "finish line".

Once you have created your basic outline, you want to include even more information in it. This would include settings where each scene takes place, the emotions behind each experience, and anything else that would contribute to you setting the mental image for the scene itself. By identifying as many descriptive factors about each major plot point as possible you make it easier for you to know exactly where you are working towards in each part of the story. Of course, you can always choose to alter these if the writing process brings you towards a different idea or plot point, but having them identified and a rough outline created can help you stay on track and remain focused on what you want to take place within' the story.

If you are someone who tends to need tools such as outlines to help you stay focused and guide you through the process it is a good idea that you complete one before you start writing any part of your novel. Having the outline written and in front of you can help you identify what you like about the story and any issues that you may notice before you actually begin writing. This can help you finalize what your conflict will be an anchor in any specific details that you want to include in your writing so that you go into your novel with a clear plan and an idea of how you are going to achieve what you have set out to accomplish.

If You Love Creative Freedom…

If you are the type of writer who prefers to work alongside creative freedom and who feels suffocated by the idea of having a specific plan to work with there are a few things that you can do in order to exercise your creative freedom while still creating an incredible novel. Just because you don't want to have a specific plan doesn't mean that you cannot create some form of a plan that will help you stay focused and work towards some form of goal throughout your novel.

It is important to understand that even if you prefer having creative freedom, you still need to have some form of outline in place to help you organize your plot and stay focused towards a particular goal. This will help ensure that your book flows in such a way that people will read it and easily work towards the goal with you, rather than attempting to understand why there are so many different pieces of information floating around that seem irrelevant to the book itself.

The first idea you could use is to create a vague outline for your book. This would require you to create an ideal starting point and ending point for your novel, and then fill out the inside of the outline with a few different major plot points that will help guide you from point a to point b. Unlike a complete outline, you will only include enough information to give you a general idea of what you want to include in your book. Then, you can come up with the rest as you are in the process of writing your novel. This can help you with allowing you to have creative expression while also staying focused on the purpose of your novel and working towards it while successfully bringing your reader along with you. Ultimately, it prevents the buildup of irrelevant information or you involving anything that is not necessary to the novel itself.

It will, however, allow you to pick out the details and other smaller factors as you go so that you can allow the story to flow through you naturally, rather than feeling pressured to use extremely specific points in varying areas of your story, potentially taking away from the natural flow that you have created through your creative expression.

Another method you can use is called a hindsight outline. The only two things you need to identify in the beginning of creating this outline is the starting and ending points. You should always have some form of end goal when it comes to writing a novel so that you are clear on what you are writing towards and what you need to be building up to throughout the novel. However, with a hindsight outline, you do not need to include any information beyond these two points. All you have to do is ensure that you are working towards the end goal. As you write major plot points into your story, you can then write them into your outline. This may seem irrelevant, but you will soon understand that writing them down allows you to see where you have come from and where you want to go. It ensures that each part of the plot works together towards the goal and that it makes sense towards the overall story. Doing this prevents you from forgetting about plot points, including ones that may contradict previous ones, and get a general idea of the flow of your story in retrospect, rather than in advance.

Questions to Ask Yourself

The following questions are questions you should ask yourself when you are developing your outline. This will ensure that you have a strong plan for your outline and that no details are missed out on.

1. Where is my protagonist starting?

2. Where are they at in their life in the beginning of the story?

3. Where is my protagonist ending?

4. Where are they at in their life at the end of the story?

5. What major plot points are getting me to (or have gotten me to) the goal?

6. Do these plot points make sense together?

7. Is there anywhere that this outline is weak?

8. What else could I add to my outline to make a rich reading experience?

How you choose to create the outline for your story is unique to you and your writing preferences. Know that you are not required to create a detailed or complete outline before you begin writing your novel. However, having an outline is extremely important as it helps you keep major plot points in chronological order and to ensure that they flow well together. Still, if you prefer to write it out in detail ahead of time, or if you prefer to merely identify your goal and create your outline in hindsight, that is entirely up to you. You should never let creating an outline and identifying specific details of your story hold you back from writing the story in the first place. Knowing that there are options for you to help you stay focused or open up your creative freedom as much as you need to can help ensure that you are not intimidated by the very first step of writing your book. It also helps you feel confident knowing that you can stay focused and still create an incredible book, whether you do it the conventional way or not.

Chapter 2: Your Setting

Developing the setting for your story provides you with the opportunity to have an incredible amount of creative expression. This part of the book is also one of the first times that you will begin to get very descriptive about what is going to happen within' your book. Even if you have a complete outline that is quite detailed, this will be more defined than that.

Your setting is ultimately when and where your story happens. This is something that you need to identify beforehand so that you can keep this information flowing throughout the entire story. For example, you wouldn't want to begin writing a story that was set in the 1800s and then use slang or information that was only relevant to the 2000s or later. Identifying your setting and being very specific and clear on it ensures that your entire book is written with relevance to that setting. The following information will help you identify important tips and tricks that you should pay attention to when it comes to developing your setting for your novel.

If You Only Have One Location

If you are writing a book where the story will never venture away from your primary overall location, then you want to make sure that you are very clear and specific on this location. This is where your entire book is going to be written, so you want to be very descriptive of and clear on this location by knowing exactly what is relevant to it and what is true about it.

You should identify where this location is, what sets it apart from other locations, and why you are using this location. You also want to discover what the local culture is like (specific to your time frame) and any other identifying factors that you may learn about this place. The best way to do it is to research this place as though you were going to be a tourist. Make sure that you do it specific to the time frame, which you will learn more about in a moment. For the location-specific part, however, you want to identify what types of buildings exist in this place, what they were made of, what the roads looked like, what types of wildlife and plant life exists in the area, and anything else that will help you create a graphic image in someone's mind about the location you have chosen.

Once you have identified the location, create a list that involves as many relevant descriptive phrases as you can. You want to generate ideas of how you will describe the place to people throughout the book and creating these ideas beforehand will ensure that you are not at a loss for words or repeating your descriptions throughout the book. Having this list will help you create a dynamic description that truly helps bring the book to life for your readers and prevents them from becoming bored of the same descriptions being used over and over again.

If You Have Many Locations

If you have many locations you want to essentially conduct what you did for one location, only for many. This part of the process may seem fairly straightforward, so we are not going to further explore the process for identifying each unique location. However, there are other things you need to consider when you are using many locations in your book.

First, you want to decide which location is going to be "home" for your characters. This one, in addition to the one where your characters stay in for the longest period of time, should be the ones that you know about the most. You should have plenty of describing factors that help set the scene for what home is like for your characters, as well as for what their new place of residence is like. For example, you might set the scene for home as "The Rocky Mountains: a place where the air is cool and crisp, and the mountainous view is one that cannot be done justice short of seeing it yourself. The community is warm and cozy, especially in the cold winters when snow makes it difficult just to leave your front door." Whereas the new place of residence is described as "The prairies, where the wheat grows for miles and you can see the entire story of the sky as clouds dance across the wide-open view in front of you. The communities are cheerful and bright, and you feel like there is nowhere you can't go, and nothing to stop you from getting where you want to be." You want to describe both the location as previously mentioned and go into detail about the emotion behind each location and why these emotions differ for the protagonist.

Second, you want to identify the mode of travel if any will be used in the book. You also want to become as descriptive as possible when it comes to the mode of transport. Where does the character get on and off of it? What stands out about this mode of transport and how does it contribute to the overall story? Is there anything particular that the reader should know that will help them feel as though they are genuinely walking up to, entering, riding, and exiting the mode of transport that you have chosen? Describing the transport itself in advance will help when it comes to foreshadowing and other story-telling tactics during the writing process. Rather than leaving it up to surprise you can easily blend it into your story so that it flows effortlessly with everything you have already written up until that point, and afterward.

If You Are Making Up the Location

If you are writing a fantasy novel where you are going to be making the location up, it is important that you take the time to actually create a location that makes sense. The location you create needs to be consistent and should be relevant to the story you are telling. There are a few tips when it comes to making up a location that you can consider using to help you create an incredible location for your book.

First, consider basing your location off of somewhere that already exists. If there is somewhere on the globe that resembles what you want your fantasy world to look like, consider first creating a descriptive location setting for that place and then alternating parts of it to fulfill your fantasy world. This will assist you with keeping everything relevant and consistent across your world.

If you are going to be making up the world entirely then you want to take your time. Close your eyes and picture this world in your own mind, first. Then, write as many descriptive factors as you can about the appearance of this location. Ultimately, you want the reader to see exactly what you are seeing in your mind at the time.

You want to make sure that when you are introducing readers to your fantasy world that they feel as though they are mentally stepping into it. They should be able to find enough information in your novel that they can not only step into the world, but they can also interact with it. They should know what type of wildlife - if any - exists in the world. Give them an idea of what the colors are like, how the communities are built, what the buildings themselves look like, and what smells they can find floating around in the air. Give them an idea of what objects are around the setting so that they can mentally picture them and that they truly feel as though they are living in your imaginary world alongside your characters. This will provide you with a strong fantasy setting that will ensure that your book truly is a fantastic read.

If You Only Have One Time Period

When it comes to time periods you need to be very specific and careful. You want to choose one that would make sense to and be relevant to the story you are telling. You also want to ensure that you do enough research about it that you tell the story as though it truly is set in that time frame. A painful mistake that would truly detract from the value of your novel would be one where you choose a certain time frame and then include information that is completely irrelevant to that time frame. For example, if you chose to set your romance novel in the late 1900s but included technology such as cell phones or computers, it would not make sense to the story and would take away from the reading experience.

When you are setting the time frame you want to ensure that you do plenty of research about it. You also want to research your chosen location with relevance to the time frame. What did it look like during that time frame? What was the culture like? What were the people like? How did they treat each other? What was the common slang for that era? You want to be very specific on what it truly would have been like during that time frame so that you can walk your reader through it. Give them the opportunity to feel as though they have stepped into a time portal and they are being transported into that era, whether it be in the present or in the past.

If You Have Many Time Periods

When you are writing a story that has many time periods the tactics you use to develop the setting is similar to if you are writing a story that has many locations. Essentially, you want to ensure that you are effectively researching each time period so that you can provide relevant and factual information based on each time period. You really need to stay focused on the details you are providing so that your reader can easily be walked back and forth with you without finding irrelevant or false pieces of information anywhere within' the text. The more focused and factual you are, the better. When it comes to developing many time periods in a story, there is not much more required than you repeating the research processes several times over for each time period you will write about. Something you may want to add, however, is the mode of transportation being used to transport across time periods. Be sure that you create a piece of machinery and provide enough details about it that you can explain how it works and create a graphic image of it in the minds of your readers.

If You Are Making up the Time Period

If you are making up a time period in your novel, then you need to be extremely descriptive about this time period. You should identify what the time period is, and why it does not already exist. For example, maybe you are generating your own fantasy setting on an alternate planet and Earth has yet to exist therefore the time is not yet in history. Or, perhaps you are writing one in the future and the time has not happened yet, so you are creating it yourself. You need to be able to thoroughly understand *why* you are creating this new time period so that your readers understand as well.

In addition to knowing why, you also need to make up all of the important details about the time period. What is the culture like in this time period? What form of government or authority exists? What do people speak like? Are there any slang words used that your readers may not already know? What do these slang words mean? How do people treat each other? What parts of the community are different from anything we experience in our own world? What else sets this time period apart from what you are presently living or what we already know about? You want to make sure that you go into detail beforehand about creating this time period so that when it comes to the writing process you already know. Doing this will ensure that you stay consistent with your novel and that nothing is added that is then forgotten about and later contradicted. When you are making something up entirely it is important that you put the effort in towards making it truly believable for your readers. This will ensure that they are able to follow the story and that it flows well without having any contradictions, confusing pieces of information, or other additions that otherwise take away from the quality of the story itself.

Combining the Two

The setting of your story is a combination of the time period and the location. When you have completely researched or created each the location and the time period, you must then combine the two. This part of the process is simple, but it is important. You want to make sure that you identify anywhere in the combination where information might contradict itself or take away from the reading experience. For example, if you are writing a book set in the present about an Amish colony that still operates without running water or electricity, you need to identify these factors and explain the discrepancy. Making sure that your time and location mesh together seamlessly and that anything contradictory is explained will ensure that you have a strong setting for your story. This means that you will be able to easily and effortlessly guide your readers through the book without any part of it leading to them wondering what is truly going on with your story.

Questions to Ask Yourself

The following questions are questions you should ask yourself when you are developing your setting. This will ensure that you have a strong plan for your setting and that no details are missed out on.

1. What location(s) will my story take place in?

2. What is unique to this location?

3. How could I describe this location in five sentences or less?

4. When I read that description, can I truly see the location in my mind?

5. Are there any further descriptions I could use to strengthen the visual of my location?

6. What time period(s) will my story take place in?

7. What is unique to this time period?

8. How could I describe this location in five sentences or less?

9. When I read that description, can I truly feel and sense the time period in my mind?

10. Are there any further descriptions I could add to enrich the time period in my story?

11. Do my time period and location make sense together?

12. What describing factors can I use to explain any

    discrepancies between my location and time period,

    if there are any?

Chapter 3: The Point of View

The next part of writing your story requires you to consider which point of view you want to write from. As an author, you have the opportunity to decide exactly how the reader is going to learn about different elements of your story, as well as how those elements will feel to them. You can do this directly through the use of point of view and which you choose to write your story in.

There are a few different points of view that you can write from when it comes to storytelling. Each one has a unique element that allows you to elaborate on and recall experiences within' the story in a certain way. Some will limit you to only telling it from one perspective whereas others allow you to elaborate with multiple perspectives, or even to provide "outsiders" insight into different experiences. How you choose your point of view will also depend on a few things. Before you choose one, however, let's explore each unique point of view and the advantages and disadvantages it provides you with as a storyteller.

First Person

First person point of view is one of the most popular choices when it comes to writing novels. This is the point of view where the writer refers to the narrator as "I", "we", "me", "mine", "my", and "us". This is similar to if you were telling a story from your own past to someone who was standing in front of you. When you are telling a story from the first-person point of view you must pick which protagonist is going to be the storyteller in your book. Typically, it is the heroic character or the one that is involved in the majority of the scenes that will be chosen as the first-person narrator. However, you can choose virtually anyone you want, dependent upon who is going to be the best angle for you to speak from.

When you write in the first person, you provide a very natural flow to your story. Your reader will feel as though you are telling them *your* story, and if you can effectively captivate them then it will actually begin to feel like your reader is the narrator. Using "I" sentiments and first-person narrative allows your reader to fully immerse themselves in the novel and get a true, deep insight into how the narrator was feeling during each scene. You also only have to pay attention to and fully develop the mind of one character: the narrators. This is the one that you will need to have the most insight to. The rest will be based on how the narrator perceives them, which means that you don't have to go quite as deep or know every minute detail of each person. However, this can also lead to some disadvantages. For example, you are limited to only reflecting on and elaborating the story based on what the narrator would feel. You cannot explore anyone else's feelings unless you use tactics such as conversation to help the narrative character explore the feelings and thoughts of another. While this is an effective tactic, you aren't going to be able to use it in every single scene or the story will sound strange and unnatural. Furthermore, the narrative character must always be involved in or at the center of every event that takes place in the book. Otherwise, large portions are going to be missed or you are going to bounce between different points of view which is not effective.

Some ways that people have managed to use the first-person narrative while still maintaining the insights on several characters at once is by developing books whereby each chapter or section is narrated by a different character. This provides the reader with the opportunity to see into several different characters and their experiences, but it can also jolt the flow of your story and result in your readers struggling to really connect with each character the way they could if you maintained a single first-person narrative.

Second Person

Second person is an undesirable choice when it comes to writing fiction, but some people choose to use it when they are writing short stories. This is an interesting point of view to write from, but it rarely creates the ability for an author to produce an entire novel without the novel sounding strange and lacking natural flow. Second person is the "you" narrative, whereby you refer to the person reading or the narrator as "you". For example, "you were standing on a street corner when suddenly someone bumped into you." The entire book would be written in this point of view which, as you might be able to tell, is not ideal. While some books have been written this way, most publishers advise against it and will even refuse to publish books that have been written in this narrative.

The only advantage to writing in the second person narrative is that your book will be unique and eccentric. Based on the nature of this narrative you gain the ability to speak directly to the reader which can be an interesting technique, but it also does not offer you a strong advantage in storytelling. For the most part, anything written in the second person narrative that is longer than a few hundred words feels uncomfortable and sounds "off" to the reader. They will likely grow tired of the eccentric feel and simply begin feeling as though the writing is uncomfortable and strange. Furthermore, it says that you are unprofessional and are inexperienced when it comes to novels. Unless you are a highly experienced writer who has already developed a name for themselves, it is typically best that you avoid this point of view.

Third Person

Third person is the point of view whereby someone completely outside of the story is telling it. For example, using identifiers such as "he" or "she" instead of "I" or "you". This point of view is another popular one when it comes to writing fiction novels because it provides the author with the ability to provide insight into many different elements of each character. It also provides the author with a greater ability to influence the reader's emotions towards various characters without that influence being limited to what would be true and natural for any given character within' the book. For example, perhaps the protagonist hates the antagonist for something he's done wrong. In the first person, you would be required to establish feelings of hatred towards the antagonist. In the third person, however, you can further explain the situation and provide the reader with insight as to how it was a mistake and the protagonist was carrying a grudge over something that was a misunderstanding, for example. It provides you with a stronger power to shape and influence the story in a highly unique way.

When it comes to writing in the third party there are two different types you can write in: third person limited omniscience, or third person unlimited omniscience. Since each one is so unique, we are going to explore them in two different subsections below.

Before we dive in, however, please note that in the following subsections we will discuss a tool many authors use whereby they speak in the third person from a different character's point of view in each scene or chapter. This helps naturally break up the story without confusing the reader along the way. This should not be confused with the technique whereby authors write one chapter per character from the first-person point of view. Although the techniques are virtually the same, they do involve writing from a different point of view in each style.

Third Person Limited Omniscience

Third person limited omniscience means that the author has the power to enter the mind of only a few characters within' the novel. Usually, during this type of experience, the author would write from the point of view of one character per chapter or per scene to avoid confusion. When it comes to this viewpoint, the author would still write with the "he" or "she" descriptors, but would primarily focus on one character per scene or chapter.

This point of view provides the author with the opportunity to enrich the experience by providing viewpoints from many different characters, thereby giving the reader a greater amount of detail and depth into each scene and experience within' the book. It also provides the author the opportunity to write from a broader scope where they are not required to limit their story to a single person's experiences. Instead, you can elaborate on experiences that may take place without one or more of the character's present. The biggest disadvantage of this is that for the author it requires you to take more time to make each part of the book flow naturally, as well as to provide distinctive voices for each character so as not to confuse yourself or your reader. Furthermore, if you switch too often you will break up the flow of your story and create an unnatural and uncomfortable. It is important that you take your time and truly dedicate if you are going to use this practice, also. Many authors find that they write in this point of view for a few chapters and then they wind up writing from the first-person narrative for the remainder of the book. This laziness can result in your first chapters, or last chapters needing to be repaired so that the entire book is written in the same narrative and flows smoothly.

Third Person Unlimited Omniscience

Third person, unlimited omniscience is virtually the same as limited omniscience, except that the author is not restricted to only sharing the experience from a few character's points of view. Instead, they can shift into the mind of any character within' the story and provide their viewpoint on the events that are taking place.

While this may provide the author with the opportunity to elaborate and provide great detail and depth to the story, it can also result in them getting far too carried away if they are not careful. Writing from too many different points of view can diffuse the entire story and result in the author washing out any storyline that may have taken place. It is similar to the mistake of oversharing or otherwise providing far too much information, well beyond what the reader needs to know. Although it may give them a strong understanding of each scene, it can also cause for it to take far too long to "get to the point already". It is generally advised against the idea of you writing in third person unlimited omniscience unless you are using the technique strategically to avoid damaging your storyline.

How to Choose

There is one incredibly each tactic to use when it comes to deciding which point of view you want to use when it comes to sharing your story. Consider taking one small scene from the book and then writing that scene in three different narratives: first person, third person limited omniscience, and third person unlimited omniscience. Only write a few short paragraphs in each point of view so that it doesn't take too long, but be sure that you write them well. Then, read each one. This will give you an idea as to how each point of view would shape the reader's experience and what "feel" it gives to your story. It also provides you with some practice as to how each point of view feels as the author and if it gives you the ability to express yourself in the way that you want to be expressed.

Questions to Ask Yourself

The following questions are questions you should ask yourself when you are choosing your point of view. This will ensure that you have a strong plan for your point of view and that no details are missed out on.

1. Who do I want to tell my story?

2. What feeling do I want my readers to have?

3. Which point of view is going to be reasonable for me to write an entire novel in?

4. Will this give me the opportunity to express my
    story the way I want to?

5. Is there any way that this might limit my story or
    otherwise hinder the reader's experience?

Chapter 4: Characters

Naturally, your story needs characters. After all, what story are you telling if there is no one taking part in the story itself? Creating a strong story requires for you to have strong, well-developed characters involved. If you are looking for greater insight as to how you can develop well-rounded characters I encourage you to read book 6 from this series: *"Character Development*: Step-by-Step."* Because I provide you with such great detail on how to develop your characters in that novel, I will not go into elaborate detail on character development in this chapter. Instead, we are going to identify other important information about your characters, such as who needs to be involved in the story and how they contribute. Knowing this basic information is powerful in regard to the actual writing process. This will help you when it comes to outlining and creating a plan for the direction of your story. When it comes to the actual writing process, however, you will want to make sure that you have fully developed characters so that they are realistic and can add to your story in a powerful way. In the meantime, let's explore other important aspects of characters in your story.

The Value of Your Characters

Characters are a powerful element of your story because they truly drive the story forward. Without characters, the story simply cannot move forward because there would be nothing to talk about. Your characters help you not only convey the story but also express it in certain ways. Depending on what point of view you have chosen, your characters can be used in unique ways to manipulate the reader's thoughts and feelings about other characters, as well as about the storyline and events that take place within' the story.

Think of professional dancers. Music is put on as the foundation for the story and it can be related to the setting. The words that coincide with the music, or the song lyrics, are responsible for providing you with insight into what the song is about. Once the dancers begin dancing, however, they can manipulate how you feel about the song, what emotions are provoked within' you, and how you take in the experience as a whole. Without the dancers, it would simply be a song with lyrics. With the dancers, it is a story with a soul.

The same goes with writing books. The setting is the foundation for your story, and the narrator is the one who tells the story. Your characters, however, provide the heart and soul of your story. They are the ones that you can use to help manipulate the readers' thoughts and provoke different emotions in them so that they experience the book in the way that you want them to. While each unique reader may have a slightly different experience, the overall interpretation of the book will remain fairly similar if you use your tools or characters, properly.

Choosing Your Protagonist

Because of how important characters are, it is vital that you choose a good character to be your protagonist. Your protagonist needs to be a strong character who can lead the story in a powerful way. When you are putting together the outline and idea for your story, consider which specific character would be best at bringing readers through the story in an effective manner that would allow you to create the experience you want to create. Which of your characters will be involved in the most experiences? Which ones will have the best emotional attachment to the storyline so that they can move your readers for you? If you are writing from a first-person narrative, you need to choose a single character that is going to be able to effectively move everyone through the entire novel. For example, it may be the wife, best friend, teacher, and book club host. Because this particular character is involved in so many different elements of the community she may be the best individual and voice to help you tell the story with a great level of depth and dynamic so that the reader truly has an incredible experience. If you are writing in the third party, however, make sure that you choose powerful characters that you will write from. These would-be ones that all connect in one way or another and that have stories that will link together. This ensures that each character makes sense to the narrative. If you are writing in third-party unlimited omniscience, make sure that when you move to the narrative of someone who may be new or unique to a specific part of the story that this move makes sense and it is clear to the reader as to why you are doing this. This will ensure that you are drawing the reader through a clear and logical storyline that makes sense.

How Many Characters Do You Really Need?

The number of characters you choose to have in your story is really unique to the story you are trying to tell. If you are telling a romance novel, for example, you may only have two primary characters and a handful of other characters that contribute to the story. For example, some best friends, family members, the cashier at the drug store they always stop at, or the receptionist at the hotel where they celebrate their honeymoon. When you are planning your story, you need to consider how many characters are actually going to be required in order for you to tell the story. As you carry on you may discover that you need to add more characters along the way, so it is not mandatory for you to identify every single character you are going to write about immediately. However, you should have a good idea of who your primary and secondary characters are going to be. Remember, your primary characters are the ones that show up in nearly all scenes and your secondary ones are characters that are recurring in a major way.

What Your Characters Say About Your Book

The characters you choose are going to say a lot about the book you are writing and the story you are telling. These characters have the power to shape the reader's perception of the book, as well as gain an even deeper insight as to what the setting is like and the feelings they should be deriving from the general information you are providing. For example, if you are writing a book from the late 1990's about a town in the southern states, you could write about a wealthy family or a poor family. This would shape your character's point of view on the entire setting and emotions associated with the book, as well as how they perceive your characters. It also helps round out your story. The characters you choose, how you design them, and how you portray them will all contribute to the story you tell. In the previous example, one story might provide the reader with a country glamorous feeling where they ride horses and own a large farm with stable hands, whereas the other might provide your family with a poorer country feel where they *are* the stable hands and they live in a shack built on the corner of the property. Who you choose for your characters will provide greater depth for your story and ultimately be the final factor that provides your reader with the clear picture of what they see, think, and feel as they read the story you have written for them.

Questions to Ask Yourself

The following questions are questions you should ask yourself when you are developing the basic outline for your characters. This will ensure that you have a strong plan for your character development and that no details are missed out on. Remember to check out book 6 where we go deeper into the creation and development of characters so that you have a strong selection of characters to help move your story forward.

1. What story am I telling and who is the focus of the story?

2. What point of view am I writing in and whose point of view do I want to write from?

3. What recurring characters are an important element of this story?

4. Are there any additional characters that will be involved in key plot points?

5. How do these specific characters help move the story?

Chapter 5: Conflict

Every good novel comes with a fair amount of conflict involved. If there was no conflict, then there would be nothing that really keeps the reader engaged. Everyone loves a great happy-ending story, but most like to see the work that goes into creating that happy ending. This is somewhat like providing a realistic snippet of your character's lives to your readers. No one's real life is easy all of the time, so writing an entire novel where all of your characters never experience any true conflict is not only unrealistic but also boring. It takes away from the entire reading experience by never giving any depth or diversity to your story.

Creating conflict in your novel should be an ongoing process. It is not simply about having one major conflict and everything being sunshine and rainbows up until and after that point. Instead, it is about leading up to the conflict, and about coming down from it as well. You want to have one primary conflict that drives the story, but you should include many other conflicts along the way as well. These smaller conflicts add more depth and reality to your story, but they also help you lead your reader through many triumphs and victories with the characters. Each time your character overcomes something your reader will feel as though they overcame it together and it will bond the reader to your character even more. Furthermore, it stops you from writing an unrealistic story that goes from bad to much worse and then suddenly great again. It provides you with a natural and lifelike flow that allows your reader to feel as though they are genuinely connecting with an individual and not a character that you have made up for the purpose of writing a novel.

Types of Conflict

There are a couple of different types of conflict that exist in every novel. The first one is considered a primary conflict. This is the primary purpose of why you are telling the story, and it is what you will lead up to and wind down from throughout the process of writing the novel. This is the "big one" that will keep your readers engaged and have them feeling like they *need* to know what happens after that particular conflict takes place.

The next type is secondary conflict. This is the type of conflict that takes place leading up to and after the primary conflict. These are smaller conflicts that exist in addition to the primary conflict. For example, maybe in an action-based novel the kidnapper is about to drive a car off of a bridge, so the protagonist has to go save the person who has been kidnapped, but they can't do that until they can get a car because the kidnapper has their car. Here, the kidnapper driving off the bridge would be the primary conflict and the lack of a car would be the secondary conflict. In the grand scheme of the entire story, however, both would be secondary to the greater problem which is that someone has been kidnapped. When you build on the conflict in this way it diversifies everything and adds a more realistic and compelling story base that drives readers forward. Now, they want to know where the protagonist gets the car from if they reach the kidnapper on time, and how they save the person who has been kidnapped. As you can see, it would keep them engaged.

The third type of conflict is an alternate conflict. In a story where third person point of view is used, the author may choose to have two or three primary conflicts going on. For example, for the parents getting divorced might be the primary conflict, for one kid her social life falling apart might be the primary conflict, and for the second kid choosing which parent to live with might be the primary conflict. This story would run with each of these conflicts equally as important as the other, and each one drives part of the story forward until it all reaches an ending whereby everyone is satisfied and happy with the outcome.

When the Conflict Should Occur

Choosing when the conflict should occur in your book is important. There are many different points at which you might desire to put the primary conflict into your plotline. However, it is imperative that you give your reader a reason to care by infusing some form of conflict into the first ten pages.

Some authors choose to start out within' the first ten pages by introducing the primary conflict and then providing the remainder of the wind-down story from there. For example, elaborating further on the plotline where someone is kidnapped, you may write that said person was kidnapped on the first page, or within' the first ten pages. The rest of the book would then be a series of secondary conflicts that result from the primary conflict, until the end where the person is rescued.

Other authors do not want to reveal the primary conflict right away and choose to save it for later. Some prefer to put it somewhere in the middle of the book and provide a fairly even amount of writing leading up to the conflict and winding down from it, whereas others like to put it towards the end of the story and use the winding down process as the opportunity to introduce the "happily ever after" experience.

Where you prefer to put the conflict in your own story heavily depends on how quickly you want your readers to move through the conflict, as well as how you want the conflict to leverage the story overall. If you want it to be the primary focus of the story, you may want to introduce it sooner or at least use secondary conflicts to suggest it starting right away. However, if you want the happily-ever-after story to be the primary focus of the story then you may want to use more casual secondary conflicts to keep the reader engaged while building them up to the conflict and then using the resolution as your final happily-ever-after scene.

Regardless of how you choose to infuse the story with your conflict, one thing remains consistent: you need to give the reader a reason to continue reading your book. Within' the first ten pages your reader needs to understand why they should fall in love with the book through developing relationships with the characters, understanding the importance of the conflicts and how they affect the characters, and what they can expect to feel when reading the book. All of this can be done by how you introduce the conflict, and when.

Questions to Ask Yourself

The following questions are questions you should ask yourself when you are developing your conflict. These questions will ensure that you are clear on what your conflict is and how it affects the story you are telling.

1. What is the primary conflict taking place in my novel?

2. How many primary conflicts do I want involved in my novel? (Note: if you are telling a story from the first person, choose one or two at most.)

3. What type of secondary conflicts can I use to build up to the primary conflict?

4. What secondary conflicts would work well to help me wind down from the conflict?

5. How do I want the conflict to drive my novel forward?

6. When do I want to introduce the conflict and how will that affect the reading experience?

7. Does the conflict make sense to the novel?

8. Does the conflict provide enough reason for the reader to truly care?

9. If I am not introducing my primary conflict right away, what conflict can I use to compel my reader to continue reading?

Chapter 6: Additional Tips

In addition to the basics of writing your novel, there are many additional tips that you can use when it comes to generating a high-quality fiction-based novel that will not only impress yourself but your audience as well. Using these tips when you are writing your story will help you increase the joy you get from the process while also increasing the value of your work. These tips are selected from a series of professional writers and have helped them in the process of generating their own fiction novels. Remember, however, not everyone is the same and therefore you may not require all of these tips when it comes to writing your own novel. Take what feels right for you and your unique story and leave the rest!

As mentioned in the introduction of this book, the tips and information provided within' this book is unique and issued to help you not only create higher quality materials but also enjoy the process. Writing your novel should be an experience that you gain joy from, not one that stresses you out or makes you feel incompetent. If you are struggling, you are not doing it right. The following tips can help take you out of the struggling mode and put you back in the mood to enjoy the experience. When the process is light and enjoyable you will likely find that you produce much better work, so be sure to slow down and readdress your approach if you are struggling to produce the results you desire.

Finally, because of the fact that some of these tips may not apply to the unique book you are writing, you will likely want to keep this information handy for any additional projects you may desire to accomplish. Some of these tips may be more relevant to certain types of books than they are to others, therefore you are likely to find value in new and unique ways each time you return to this book.

Think Outside of the Box

When it comes to writing stories, there are many plotlines that exist that are simply rewritten with different angles and different characters. The setting may be different and some of the events that take place may alter, but ultimately the entire story works out to be similar to several other books within' the same genre. Although the saying "don't try to reinvent the wheel" may ring true in many cases, it is not always the best approach to take when you are attempting to write a new and interesting book that will engage your readers in a powerful way.

Instead of trying to recreate a tired plotline, try thinking outside of the box entirely. Consider the genre you are writing for, such as romance, mystery, or fantasy, and spend some time thinking about parts of the story that are never typically told within' traditional novels from that genre. As you discover new parts of the story that you can emphasize on, make sure that you are truly criticizing them to ensure that there is a good reason as to why this part of the story hasn't been told before. Sometimes a certain element may be rejected or ignored because there simply isn't enough to talk about, other times it may be because that isn't the traditional approach, therefore, most people don't consider it when they are writing a novel in that genre.

Looking at things from a different perspective and discovering new ways to share a story provides your book with a unique twist that allows you to engage your readers not only through incredible work but also through the element of surprise. For example, most romance novels lead up to the part where the lovers fall in love, but what if your novel was more focused on the wind-down? What if the marriage happened within' the first ten pages and from there it was the wind-down and told the next part of the romance story that most novels don't focus on? Paying attention to unique elements of the story gives you the opportunity to still write in your chosen genre while also having the chance to put a unique spin on things and create a story that people weren't expecting.

Ditch Expectations

When it comes to the writing world you will likely stumble on expectations from many different people. Publishers, readers, yourself, other authors, everyone has an expectation of what a book "should" be like. While it is important to consider these elements, especially since some of them can make or break the success of your book, it is also important to ditch the pressure that comes along with them.

Most writers can agree that feeling too much pressure can result in writer's block and it can also drown the enjoyment you gain from writing the book. It can make it feel too much like work and less like an experience to be enjoyed by both you and the readers. Instead of putting that much pressure on yourself, ditch expectations and write for the trashcan. You will likely be surprised at the quality of work you produce when you aren't considering all of the technical aspects of your book.

Set Deadlines

Having deadlines set in place can help you keep motivated, and it can also help you plan for other parts of the book writing process. For example, this can help you decide when you need to begin approaching publishers when work needs to be handed in, when marketing efforts should commence, and more. Having deadlines in place keeps everything moving forward and prevents you from avoiding or neglecting your book altogether.

When you are setting deadlines, however, be generous with yourself. Do not set a deadline that is fixed on a date that requires you to work an obscene amount each day from where you are now until the deadline arrives. Doing this will bring back the pressure and take away the joy of the writing experience. Instead of writing and allowing the story to flow through you, you will be writing under the pressure of knowing that if you don't get a certain amount of words out *right now* that you will officially be late for your deadline and everything will be hindered by your lack of writing speed. Instead, choose a generous deadline that gives you plenty of time to take breaks, step aside and get a breather, and come back to your work to finish it. Be kind to yourself and account for breaks. Most writers do not write an entire book in one straight shot. Instead, they write for several days, or even weeks, and then take breaks off in between to allow for more inspiration to come to them before they carry on. Give yourself the opportunity to have these breaks so that you can take them without feeling pressure.

Get a Good "Test" Reader

When your book is complete, you need to have a good test reader who can read through it for you. This is someone who is not necessarily looking for grammatical errors or otherwise editing your book. Rather, they are simply reading to see if it is engaging and if it will actually appeal to your audience. Naturally, this person should identify with your target audience or their opinion may not count for much.

It is important that you do not hand your book to everyone you know and get as many people as possible. Instead, pick one or *maybe* two test readers who identify with your target audience and allow them to read the book. This way you can get honest opinions without feeling overwhelmed by a number of responses you get. It also helps open your purchasing audience because your friends and family will likely be some of your earliest buyers once your title is launched.

Avoid Perfectionism

Many writers put a pressure on themselves to create the perfect piece of work. They may think of an artist they already know or a series of books they have read that they perceive as perfect and they want their books to be the same quality. Understand that this is not valuable to the writing process and it can actually hold you back from producing high-quality work.

Perfectionism can be intimidating, and it can have you overly critical of the work you are producing. Most of the best books that exist on shelves today were not subjected to perfectionism. Instead, the author focused on telling a great story, not a perfect one. Readers are not expecting a perfect book, they are expecting one that takes them through the story in such a way that is engaging and makes them genuinely feel as though they are present and can relate to what they are reading. Perfectionists need not worry.

Write What You Don't Know

There is a long-standing piece of advice that tells writers to "write what they know", but this isn't always the best way to go. Unless you are deeply passionate about your topic and can infuse it with all of the emotions related to that passion, consider writing what you *don't* know.

Think about a topic that interests you and things you would have to learn based on that new interest. Then, spend time researching it for the purpose of writing the book. For example, if your protagonist is a karate star, consider going to a few karate lessons to get a first-hand idea of what it is like so that you can write from within' the experience. Writing in this way gives you a better opportunity to convey the excitement that you are feeling through your story, thus translating it into the reader's experience.

When we write about what we know, we often don't have the same level of excitement or passion as we would if we were brand new to the knowledge because we have a "been there, done that" feeling towards the topic. Even when we are passionate about it, it can be hard to convey that new childlike wonder through the story. When you are brand new, however, it is brand new to you *and* the reader, and it can enhance the quality of your story through all of the exciting emotions you infuse it with.

Manipulate Your Reader's Emotions

Readers are most often attracted to books that draw out a variety of emotions in them. You want to use your characters and the storyline to manipulate your reader's emotions so that they are emotionally drawn to and attached to the book as you are reading. Many readers agree that the best books are the ones that leave you with a "lost" feeling when you put them down. This is because the reader has developed an emotional attachment to the book, likely based on the writer's technique.

You can manipulate your reader's emotions through a variety of different plot points, experiences, and descriptive phrases. You want to start by helping them become emotionally connected to one or more of the characters, then subject these characters to various experiences that draw out certain emotions in the characters. As a result, it will draw out emotions in your readers as well.

When your reader is emotionally connected to the book, they are far more engaged and much more likely to read it all the way through. Furthermore, they are much more likely to genuinely enjoy the book. Make sure that you play with several different emotions so that the book is not excessively sad, angry, funny, or otherwise. Even if you want to emphasize on one emotion more than the rest, be sure to add a healthy mixture of other emotions so that the book does not become predictable or boring.

Conclusion

Thank you for reading *"How to Write a Novel: Step by Step | Essential Romance Novel, Mystery Novel and Fantasy Novel Writing Tricks Any Writer Can Learn"*!

I hope that this book was able to provide you with many tips and tricks to assist you in the process of writing your very own fiction novel. Whether you are writing a romance novel, a mystery novel, or a fantasy novel, I hope that you were able to learn many valuable methods to increase the enjoyment of the experience and increase the quality of your work overall. This book was designed to help you master the writing process, and I hope that you were able to learn plenty of new and diverse information in order to help you do so.

The next step is to start writing! If you haven't already, begin with your outline and move forward from there. As you are working on your book, be sure to check back with this guidebook regularly to see if there are any tips or tricks related to the part of the process you are presently in. This book was written to be a writing resource that you can check back to as often as you need, so don't hesitate to keep it handy during the entire writing process. You never know what part of the book might become valuable to you during each unique part of the process!

Thank you, and enjoy!

OUTLINING

STEP-BY-STEP

ESSENTIAL CHAPTER OUTLINE, FICTION AND NONFICTION OUTLINING TRICKS ANY WRITER CAN LEARN

BOOK 2: OUTLINING

STEP-BY-STEP

Essential Chapter Outline, Fiction and Nonfiction Outlining Tricks Any Writer Can Learn

Sandy Marsh

reparation, damages, or monetary loss due to the information herein, either directly or indirectly.

Respective authors own all copyrights not held by the publisher.

The information herein is offered for informational purposes solely, and is universal as so. The presentation of the information is without contract or any type of guarantee assurance.

The trademarks that are used are without any consent, and the publication of the trademark is without permission or backing by the trademark owner. All trademarks and brands within this book are for clarifying purposes only and are the owned by the owners themselves, not affiliated with this document.

Table of Contents

Introduction... **78**

Chapter 1: The Basics of Making an Outline....................... **80**

What is an outline? 80

Who uses an outline? 81

The importance of using an outline 82

Outlining for fiction vs. Non-fiction........................... 84

Plot outline vs. synopsis... 85

Understand the plot of a story 86

Why is it important to understand the plot?................... 90

Chapter 2: Fiction Outline **91**

Snowball Method 91

Pure summary 93

Skeletal outline 95

Bullet outline.. 98

Chapter outline 101

Sequence outline 102

Flowchart outline 104

Visual outline 105

Chapter 3: Non-Fiction Outline 107

Pure summary 107

Skeletal outline 109

Bullet outline 110

Chapter outline 112

Research 115

Chapter 4: Best Practices 116

Know your characters 116

Know your story 118

Keep it simple 119

Be flexible 120

Have a clear premise 123

Take a break 125

Choose and organize your ideas 126

Observe proper sequence 127

Focus on the main points 128

It does not have to be perfect 129

Remember that an outline is just a guide 131

Take your time 132

Have your sources ready 133

Ask yourself questions 135

Practice.. 137

Conclusion **140**

Introduction

Congratulations on purchasing this book and thank you for doing so. The following chapters will teach you all the important things that you need to know about making an outline. Learning to make an effective outline is an invaluable tool as a writer. It can help the writing of your book to flow more smoothly, work out more conveniently and be organized.

Chapter 1 talks about the basics of making an outline. This will give you a good foundation and understanding of what outlining is all about. Chapter 2 discusses how you can make an outline for a fiction book. Chapter 3 teaches how you can make an outline for a non-fiction book. Chapter 4 lays down the best practices that you should observe when making an outline.

Writing a book can be a daunting task. By using an outline, you can make the process of writing a book simpler and easier. The good news is that it is not hard to make an outline as long as you know what you are doing. An outline is an effective tool and is the secret behind an effective book writing. By learning how to

make an outline, you are able to cover a significant part of the
actual book-making process. Take the outline as a blueprint, the
guide, or architecture, of your book.

Chapter 1: The Basics of Making an Outline

What is an outline?

An outline works as a guide when it comes to writing your book. Take note that a book is a big world. Without a good outline, you can easily get lost in the process of writing your book. An outline ensures that you stay within the plot that you want for your book and that every scene works towards building your story.

It is worth noting that an outline only serves as a guide. A writer has the option whether or not to stick to their outline. Still, having an outline is helpful because it will give you a sense of direction. It is also a useful tool to use to ensure proper sequencing of events or scenes in your book.

There are different ways to make an outline. This book will teach you notable and effective methods to outline a book, both for a fiction book and a non-fiction book. Indeed, learning how to make an outline is an invaluable tool that should be in the arsenal of every writer.

It can be said that an outline is the book itself but in a very simplified version. It can also deal with the technical aspects of the book, such as the timing as to when and how a certain characters or ideas will be presented. Consider the outline as the blueprint or the foundational architecture of your book.

Who uses an outline?

Almost all professional writers use an outline. Some go as far as saying that all writers *should* use an outline. The use of an outline does not just refer to books, but even in other forms of writing. In fact, it is not uncommon even for article writers to write an outline for their more complicated articles. An outline ensures that the focus of your writing and the proper flow remain concentrated. So, if making an outline is really this important, are there known authors who apply them? The answer is yes. Here are some examples to name a few: The author of *Harry Potter*, JK Rowling, James Salter, Paulo Coelho, Sylvia Plath, Jennifer

Egan, William Faulkner, and many other popular writers have admitted the use of outlines in the creation of their works. As you can see, using an outline is considered such an essential skill and tool of a writer that even well-known authors use it regularly.

Should you use an outline? Well, just because you are a writer does not necessarily mean that you are required to make an outline before writing your book. So, whether you want to use an outline or not is a matter of personal preference. Still, it is worth noting that many writers have realized the benefits of using an outline.

The importance of using an outline

It is worth noting that there are some authors who do not use an outline when they write a book. Instead, they simply allow the natural current of the work to drive them to somewhere, hoping that it would be worth telling. However, the truth is that many of these of authors have outlined the book in their mind, so somehow, they still have that sense of direction. Of course, there are also those writers who completely have no idea of what they are writing and just see where the writing goes. After all, when it comes to writing, especially when it comes to writing fiction, there are no hard and fast rules to limit a writer. You are free to write your book in whatever way you want just as you are also free not to write a book. However, if you want to be sure of your sense of direction and not waste your time writing on so many pages only to realize that they do not make sense, then you should use an outline. An outline is also easy to make, yet it will assure you that your book has a good flow and direction.

Now, there are those who say that using an outline will only limit your imagination, so they do not want to use an outline when they write a book. They do not want the outline to "cage" the expression and flow of their ideas. However, this is not the correct way to view an outline. Take note that as a writer, an outline is still just an outline. You are not in any way compelled to follow your outline all of the time. For example, let us say while you are writing the setting of the story as stated in your outline you realize that a different place would be more suitable, then you are free to use that place instead of what is in your outline. Of course, the same principle applies to the other parts of the book.

Again, an outline is a helpful guide that will ensure to give you a sense of direction; it should not, in any way, be seen as an obstacle or a cage that limits your imagination. You are strongly encouraged to stretch and explore the beauty of your mind. In fact, even an outline comes from the creative mind of a writer. The outline can be thought of as the skeleton of the book that you hang the actual story on.

Outlining for fiction vs. Non-fiction

Outlining works for any kind of book, whether fiction or non-fiction. However, making an outline for a fiction book is not the same when you make an outline for a nonfiction book and vice versa. This is because of the inherent differences between the two genres. In a fiction book, for example, a novel, you will need to spend more time outlining the plot of the story and the sequencing of the events.

You should be able to present your characters effectively and build up the story. In the case of a non-fiction book, there is usually no need to build up any story. Instead, you should focus on presenting the right information. Of course, the proper sequence should also be observed. In a fiction book, the outline will be mostly composed of the setting, the characters, and the different events that take place in the story. In a non-fiction book, the outline will be divided into main topics and subtopics regarding technical subjects.

Although there are differences between making an outline for fiction and nonfiction, the use and purpose of an outline still remain the same, and that is to make writing the book easier and more organized.

Plot outline vs. synopsis

Many people use these two terms interchangeably. However, it is worth noting that they are not the same. Take note that when you create a plot outline before even start writing a book you then use the outline as your guide as you write, so that you will be guided on how the story should flow. Writers who use plot outlines are usually called "plotters" since they plot the whole story before they even write it down. This is a good way to avoid writing too many drafts with rejected scenes and pages.

A synopsis is usually written after the completion of the book. It refers to the summary of your story or novel. The synopsis is usually a part of a proposal letter that a writer sends to a potential publisher.

A synopsis can be as short as a single page or even up to five pages. A plot outline can also take a single page but can be longer than five pages. It depends on how much you work on your outline. If you add in more details, then it will be able to guide you once you proceed to write your story. In addition to the story, a plot outline can include a detailed character story and other events.

Some writers already know their story before they even write it. So, if you can come up with the synopsis first, then you can use that as a guide to make a more detailed outline.

Understand the plot of a story

If you are into fiction writing, then it is important for you to know the plot of a story. What is a plot? It is what draws readers into the story. It refers to the arrangement of the story elements. There are generally five parts of a plot: the beginning or exposition, rising action, climax, falling action, and denouement or ending. Let us take a look at them one by one.

Exposition

The exposition is the beginning of a story. Hence, this is the part where you present your characters. Take note that the characters are not the only ones that develop your story. You also need to pay attention to the place, as well as the time. Unfortunately, some people forget about the element of time. Do not forget that Paris today was much different a hundred years ago. It is also important to keep the exposition as interesting as possible. You need to make it grab the interest of your readers; otherwise, they might stop reading your book before they even find out the about good and exciting parts.

Rising action

This is where you build up your story. This is usually where a problem is presented, and the characters take steps to face or solve the problem. This is also what prepares the most exciting part of the story, the climax. The rising action is where you build up the anxiety and the expectations. This is also the part where you start to tug at the hearts and emotions of your readers. The more attached the readers are to the characters, the more powerful the climax and the overall story will be. It is important that a writer build up the story effectively; otherwise, the story may become boring to the reader.

Climax

This is known as the turning point and the most exciting part of the story. This is where the emotions are at their peak. Nothing is ever the same as this point. This is where real and solid changes take place. Usually, immediately right after the climax, everything takes a downhill, relaxes, and prepares for the ending.

Falling action

This is the part where the story falls and takes a downhill, which leads to the ending of the story. Here, the story usually comes together, and the missing pieces are finally resolved. This is also where you reward your audience. Take note that your readers normally associate themselves with the protagonist in the story, so you use this part show them how the protagonist is rewarded for all of his or her labor. This is also a good part to impress on the readers the moral of your story if any.

Denouement

This is the ending of the story. Here, the loose ends are tied, and the questions are finally answered. Of course, it can be a happy ending or a sad ending. A story can even have an open ending where there is technically no end and you leave to the reader the final conclusion of the story.

Why is it important to understand the plot?

As a writer, it is important for you to understand the plot. When you make an outline, you actually work on the plot of your story, such as how are you going to begin the story, how do you present your characters, the time and place, etc. before then you moving on to the rising action, then the climax, and so on. As you can see, it is important to have a good understanding of the plot because the story revolves around the plot that you set. There are also writers who make an outline by simply filling in the parts of the plot with details.

Chapter 2: Fiction Outline

Snowball Method

The snowball method is one of the most popular techniques for making an outline. Just like a rolling snowball that gets bigger and bigger as it rolls downhill, the snowball method starts with just a simple topic, idea, or a scene. It will then be continuously developed, and it will branch out to more ideas, more scenes, and other parts of the story.

For example, let's start with the simple idea of a man who falls in love with a woman. Let this idea be the very center of the snowball. This will also be the main theme of the story. We now branch out a little and give them each a name. Let us say that the name of the man is Jack and the name of the woman is Mina. So now we have the protagonists of the story, as well as the central theme of love. Of course, Jack cannot just fall in love with Mina out of nowhere. So, we add another part to our snowball: let us say for example that Mina is in need of money. She then applies for a job at a nearby restaurant which happens to be owned by Jack. Let us say that Mina is able to get the job as a waitress, and she then works as a waitress gets to meet other people who work at the restaurant. Again, this is another part of the snowball.

When working as a waitress, one day, Mina encounters a very rude customer. Again, we let the snowball turn, and we simply continue to add more information or details. For example, let us say that the rude customer is the one who complains and calls for the manager of the restaurant who happens to be Jack as well, the owner. Jack then is able to put the situation under control. That evening, Jack calls Mina to his office for a meeting. Mina is anxious about it because she does not want to lose her job. Again, we simply let the snowball turn and gather more details. Contrary to what she has expected, once she is already in the office, Jack appears to be very polite and even apologizes for what happened that day.

This is simply how the snowball method works. Simply put, you just have to keep adding more and more details. If you continue to do this, then you will soon come up with a short story, a novelette, or even a novel. From one small snowball, you simply let it roll and roll and gather more ideas and details to turn it into a big snowball, a complete story. Also, do not forget that you are writing an outline and not a story just yet. So, keep it simple and short, but be sure that the main points of the story are there.

Pure summary

As the name implies, a pure summary outline is the kind of outline that is composed of summaries. This is like the short version of your entire book or novel. You simply have to summarize everything, such as chapters, scenes, and others.

The idea behind this method is to write down your whole story from beginning to end, but only write down a compressed version. To do this, just write down the important parts or highlights. You can skip all forms of dialogues and just focus on telling what is happening in the story.

For example, Ana is looking for a job and applies as a journalist. She gets the job and as she works as a journalist, she gets to meet Ryan, a photographer, who happens to work in the same company. Despite their busy schedule, they do their best to make time for each other. One day, Ana is in an accident and

Ryan does his best to serve her. To save her life, he has to go into an ancient forest and get a golden apple from a mysterious tree. He ventures into the forest and meets Galdorf, a friendly elf. Galdorf helps him find the mysterious tree and battle the Dark Witch of the forest. By doing so, he frees the imprisoned elves and also saves Ana from dying. They live happily ever after.

As you can see, every part of the story is compressed but it is complete. All that you need to do is to fill in the details. The good thing here is that you are already given a clear roadmap or guideline as to how your story will flow from start to finish. In fact, by using this approach, you will already be able to imagine your story as a whole, and all that you need to do is to write down the details to make the story come alive.

The pure summary is one of the best ways to make an outline. Just summarize every chapter or sub-chapter from beginning to end. When done, you will have a complete story. All that you need to do is to clarify every point by adding in more details.

Skeletal outline

You have probably learned this kind of outline in school or for any other academic purposes. The key to this method is to input the core points in the right order that will best present your story. This is an effective way to get a bird's eye view of your story, including its overall structure. Take note that the structure of a book or story is essential. A book that is poorly structured, whether fiction or non-fiction, will most probably have problems with being disorganized and have confusing contents. A skeletal outline will allow you to easily reform your story or book, which will allow you to create the maximum impact out of your story. Let us take a look at a simple example of a skeletal outline:

Exposition

- The setting of the story takes place in a small village called as Sestin.

- The story introduces Adam, who is a farmer.

- The story then introduces Monica, the daughter of a rich businessman

Rising action

- Adam meets Monica as he tends the farm of her father.

- They get to know each other for some days.

- One day, goblins attack the village of Sestin.

- Monica is held hostage by the goblins.

Climax

- Adam fights the goblins and saves Monica.

- The story also reveals that they both share the same mutual feeling for each other.

- It is found that Adam is actually of royal blood and owns a kingdom

Falling action

- The father of Monica allows Adam to marry his daughter

Denouement

- Adam and Monica get married and everyone is happy.

- They all live happily ever after.

Take note that this is just an example of a skeletal outline. It may be shorter or even much longer than this. The important thing is to plot the story and the events properly. It is also worth noting that this kind of outline is not just applicable to fiction writing. You can also use it for non-fiction works. This will be discussed in more detail later in the book.

A good thing about this approach is that it allows you to see the structure of your book more clearly. Usually, a skeletal outline clearly divides the book into parts and is just composed of single lines. When taken together, they all compose a whole story.

Bullet outline

- A bullet outline is one of the most common types of outlining. In fact, this is one that is widely used by people even if they do not read about it. With a bullet outline, you simply have to make notes in bullet form as to what will happen in the story. For example:

- Lisa is an accountant.

- One day, she meets Mr. Gibson, a high-stakes gambler.

- They get to know each other better.

- They fall in love with each other.

- However, Mr. Gibson's gambling addiction starts to become a problem and begins to affect their relationship.

- Lisa tries to help Mr. Gibson and does her best to save their relationship.

- (and so on and so forth)

This is an example of a bullet outline. So, how do you use this outline? It is actually fairly simple. Using the example, at first you expound on the part of the outline that says, "Lisa is an accountant." A good way to do this when you actually write your novel is to describe the nature of Lisa's work. Make it as meaningful and interesting as possible.

If you look at the next part of the sample outline, the next part is "One day, she meets Mr. Gibson, a high-stakes gambler." Of course, you would not have to write this line as is. Rather, just like the first bullet, you make it more details. How did they meet? Perhaps Mr. Gibson starts to have money problems and needs an accountant to save his business. You can explore and expound on this once you actually start to write the book. Take note that this single bullet alone can take a whole chapter. This is just to give you an example of how to use a bullet outline more effectively.

A bullet outline is a very simple yet effective method. Another benefit of using this kind of outline is that it gives you a lot of room to exercise your imagination once you start to write the story. The outline focuses more on the flow of the story instead of what is actually happening in the story.

It is common to use a bullet outline on a per chapter basis. Many writers first prepare an outline in bullet form before they begin writing a chapter. This way, they can be sure that they know the direction of the story. Every bullet point is also usually short, so it would not be hard for you to follow it. Once you have a well-established outline in bullet form, then all you need to do is fill in the details of every bullet point and not worry about the direction that your story will take.

Chapter outline

A chapter outline divides a story into chapters. Every chapter will then have an outline of what is going to happen in that particular chapter. Here is an example:

Chapter 1: The Meeting

Noah calls for all the soldiers to attend the secret meeting.

Every soldier attends the meeting, except for Jason.

Jason, the number one soldier in the world, wakes up in a hospital with amnesia.

Even though Jason is not able to attend the meeting set by Noah, Noah is soon able to follow his tracks and visits him in the hospital.

Noah reminds Jason who he really is.

As you can see from the example, the book will be divided into chapters and every chapter will then be divided into sub-topics or events that take place in the story. A chapter outline is a good method, especially if you are particular with every chapter in your book.

As is usual, only the main points are included. This is to give room for you to exercise your creative imagination when you write the story. The outline is just enough to guide you as to what will happen next and avoid the situation where you get stuck up not knowing how to make the story to flow continuously. A chapter outline is also one that is commonly used by writers.

Sequence outline

A sequence outline puts more focus upon the sequencing of the events in the story. However, it still outlines the important points, so even this method alone would be enough to help you with writing your book. Here is an example of this kind of outline:

1 - Dianne, still a very young child, is baptized as a witch.

2 - Her parents were killed for practicing sorcery.

3 - She soon grows into one of the most powerful witches.

4 - Dianne meets King Gregory, the man who had ordered for her parents to be burned at the stake.

(and so on and so forth)

As you can see, there is a fine outline of the sequence of the events. If you are the type of writer who finds it hard to stick to the flow of your story, then a sequence outline may be the one for you.

Although you can add in as many details as you want, it is important to stick to the sequence; otherwise, a change may have major effects on the story as a whole. Take note that if you mess up with even just one part of the sequence, then you should check how it affects the other parts. Are they still logical enough when taken together? This method is also commonly used by writers. It is also like a bullet form outline but is more particular with the sequence of the events and the flow of the story.

Flowchart outline

This approach makes use of a flowchart. This is similar to a sequence outline but makes use of a chart that is also in proper sequence. Here is a simple example:

Adam works as a painter --> He attends an event for artists --> While at the event, he sees and meets Stella --> He falls in love with her at first sight --> and so on and so forth.

As you can see, the scenes or parts of the chapters are reflected through this flowchart. When you finally start working on the book, then you will add in the details to every point in the chart. A single part of the flowchart can cover a few pages up to a whole chapter, depending on what is happening in your story. So, for example, let us take the first part of the flowchart: Adam works as a painter. When you write this in your book, you can then expound on this topic. You describe the nature of his work and you can also write and show what happens in his life as a painter. As you can see, just these things alone can take many pages, even a whole chapter.

The thing with a flowchart method, just like any other outlining method, is for you to pinpoint the main parts of the story and ensure that you arrange things in the right order. Once everything is set, then you simply have to add the details when you write the book.

Visual outline

If you are fond of drawing, then this style of outlining may be the one for you. When you use a visual outline, all that you need to do is to draw the main events in a story, especially its plot. Take note that instead of writing in words, this approach lies in drawing and making figures. For this, you may want to use a notebook. You can fill each page with a drawing that would illustrate what the scene will be. You then follow it up with another scene on the next page, and so on and so forth.

Even if you cannot draw well, you can still use this approach. After all, just like any other outlines, this is something that you do not need to show to anyone else. An advantage of using drawings instead of words in making an outline is that you will have more room to play with the words, as well as for the exercise of your imagination. This is because every drawing can have diverse meanings and significance. If you want a style of outline that will give you maximum use of your imagination once you begin writing your book, then perhaps using a visual outline is a good idea. However, the drawback is that this kind of outlining may not always work for everyone. In fact, the very reason why you want to make an outline is to have a good sense of direction when you finally write your book. The risk is that you may not be so inspired when you finally write your book that the drawings may start to look boring or empty to you.

Chapter 3: Non-Fiction Outline

Pure summary

Just like for fiction writing, you can also use the pure summary approach for non-fiction book writing. When you use this approach, simply make a summary of the information. This means that you do not have to explain anything. Just make a summary of every chapter in the book. For sub-topics, you can simply write a one or two-sentence summary. Again, this is just a summary, so there is no need for you to expound or explain anything. Still, it is worth noting that when you read a summary, the stories must be coherent and logical enough. In other words, it must still be a complete story with proper flow and structure. However, of course, you do not want for it to too detailed. After all, it is just a summary, which can be a summary per chapter or even per sub-topic in every chapter. The important thing is for the summary to mention the main points of the book. This will also ensure that you will not forget about them.

When you use this method, then it is also important that you pay attention to the sequence of the information. A common rule in non-fiction writing is to start from the basics, and then gradually branch out to more complicated matters on the subject.

In non-fiction, you are not expected to make a well-detailed summary considering that there is a chance that you still need to learn more specific details about the topic in question. Of course, if you know exactly what you are writing about then you may only require a minimum level of research; however, if you are writing something about which you do not have enough knowledge, then there would be little that needs to be summarized. If you want, you can just research and study the subject first before you start to make a pure summary outline. However, do not let the lack of research prevent you from using this approach. After all, you have the convenience of having open books and information both when you make an outline and when you write the book.

Skeletal outline

A skeletal outline is common in non-fiction writing, especially when the book deals with a technical topic. This is because a skeletal outline offers exactly what you would need for non-fiction writing. When you use this approach, you begin with a subtitle, which may be the name of your chapter. You then identify and specify the skeletal outline of the book with the topics and sub-topics that you will discuss in the book. Needless to say, this follows the same format as the one for fiction. However, unlike a fiction book, this does not follow any plot. Rather, it has a more logical flow to it. For example, when you write a book about bitcoin, you should not talk about bitcoin mining right away. Instead, you should start with the basics, such as what bitcoin is, what a cryptocurrency is, and others, and then make your way up from there.

Bullet outline

A bullet outline is excellent when you deal with specifics. For example, when you make an outline of a chapter or sub-chapter in a book. Also, what you can do is to highlight the name of a chapter, and then simply outline in bullet form what you want to talk about for that part of the book. For example, let us say that you want to write a book about the cryptocurrency Bitcoin, here is a sample outline:

Chapter 1: The Basics of Bitcoin

- What is Bitcoin?

- What is cryptocurrency?

- What is a cryptocurrency wallet?

- Who uses bitcoin

- How does a bitcoin transaction work?

- (and others)

As you can see, every point is made clear. All that is left for you to do is add the details. Of course, you can further use the bullet outline like this:

Chapter 1: The Basics of Bitcoin

- What is Bitcoin?

  - a digital money

  - uses cryptography

- What is cryptocurrency?

  - cryptography for secure communication and transaction

- What is a cryptocurrency wallet?

  - a place to store cryptocurrency

  - kinds of cryptocurrency wallets (hot and cold wallets)

- Who uses bitcoin

- anyone with an Internet connection

- How does a bitcoin transaction work?

  - Input

  - Recipient's wallet address

  - Amount

As you can see, this makes it more detailed and it will be easier to fill in the information once you start writing the book. When you write non-fiction, outlining your work is more practical. After all, non-fiction works do not deal so much with one's creative imagination. The important thing is for you to be able to cover the technical details and be able to present them effectively.

Chapter outline

A chapter outline is one of the simplest ways to make an outline for a non-fiction book. Basically, you simply have to write the name of the chapter, and then add in the titles of the sub-topics within a chapter. This is also like a bullet form of outlining but is more general. Of course, you can also make it more specific by further outlining the sub-topics just like in a bullet outline. In fact, both kinds of outline are very similar to each other.

The first step in a chapter outline is to set the titles of the chapters. Again, as a rule in non-fiction, you should start with the basics. The reason is that you must first establish a foundation for your readers before you delve into more complicated matters. A common mistake committed by writers is to assume that the reader already knows and understands the topic. If you come to think of it, this understanding is highly flawed. After all, a reader would not have to waste time reading your book if he is already aware or if he already understands what is written in your book. So, never assume that the reader can easily understand what you write. Instead, have an open mind and consider the reader as someone who knows nothing about your subject. Of course, this is subject to some exceptions, for example, if you target readers are really those who already have an idea of your subject. A good example of this will be the advanced guides or manuals.

Once you have the titles of the different chapter ready, then it is time for you to add in the subtitles that will be placed under each corresponding chapter. You should be careful about the subtitles because they are the ones that will lead the development of the book. Hence, they are the ones that will form the structure of the book. Just stick to the basic rule of starting with the basics and then work your way up, and you will be fine. This is just a matter of presentation. Feel free to try different combinations until you find the one that feels most natural and convenient for a reader.

The number of chapters will depend on the kind of book that you write, as well as the number of words of the entire book. Normally, the longer the book is, the more chapters it will include. When you write your outline, be sure to pay attention to how many chapters your book will have, as well as the number of sub-topics that you will be using. It helps if you have more sub-topics so that you will not run out of things to write about. However, take note that book writing is not about the length but the quality if your book. Hence, it is important that you focus more on the quality of your writing that on the number of chapters or subtitles that your book has.

Research

Although not considered as a complete outlining method, when it comes to non-fiction writing, research is the main tool that you have in your arsenal. Although you are still free to use your imagination, non-fiction writing has certain restraints upon one's writing. The golden rule is that you cannot contradict a fact. Well, except, of course, if you have another set of facts to present that can support your view. Take note that when it comes to non-fiction writing, the facts are your friends. Needless to say, in a non-fiction book, almost everything that you write should be backed up by research or at least verifiable. This is to make your writing more believable and credible.

In non-fiction writing, it does not matter how good your outline is if you do not understand the subject. Hence, make sure that you have all the necessary materials to get to know your subject and do as much research as possible. The more that you know your subject, the easier it will be for you to come up with a good outline, and the easier it will be for you to complete the book.

Chapter 4: Best Practices

Know your characters

When you write a story, especially in fiction writing, it is important for you to know your characters. It is worth noting that an outline is not something that you use to get to know your characters. It is important for you to know the characters first before you make an outline.

Take note that the characters are important as they are the ones that tell and develop the story. If there are not enough characters or if you do not know your characters well enough, then the story will not grow properly. Therefore, is important for you to know and understand who your characters are. In fact, once you know your characters, then telling the story will come naturally as the characters themselves will play out the story. This is the part of writing a story where the writer becomes a mere observer of his characters. You can allow your characters to lead you. This will give you an idea of what the story will be and, so it will be easier for you to make an outline.

If you do not know your characters yet, especially your main characters in the story, then you should give yourself more time to get to know them. You do not necessarily have to know all your characters completely. You will know if you already have sufficient understanding of your characters when the characters themselves are able to lead and create the story for you. Needless to say, every character must have his or her own persona and should act according to that personality.

A suggested way to know your characters is to interview them one by one. This is a common practice used by novel writers. So, how does it work? Just imagine talking to your character. Ask them questions and see and feel how they respond. This may seem strange to some people, but many writers use this approach. They talk to their characters to the point like they feel that they are merely recording (writing) what the characters in the story are telling them. Once characters are given a persona and existence in the story, it will seem that they really have an identity and life of their own. Hence, talk with your characters and ask them questions. Learn from them. This way you will be more able to develop your story.

Know your story

Take note that your plot is like the skeleton of your story. Therefore, when you write a plot it is also important that you already have an idea of what your story is going to be. When you write an outline, it is not important for you to know the minor details and the dialogues of the characters. However, it is important for you to know the main points of your story or the main events that will shape your story. These are the things that will constitute your outline.

The more that you know your story, the easier it will be for you to make an outline of it. After all, making an outline is as simple as recording essential details and skipping dialogues and other things that are considered important to a novel. It is more focused on simply having a worthwhile story instead of discussing all the things that happen in a story.

Now, it is also worth noting that many writers write an outline even without knowing their story. How is this possible? Well, they allow the process of outlining to reveal the story to them. To do this, you just need a basic idea. You write it down as part of an outline, and then simply add more details to it to continue to grow your idea. Since you are just making an outline, it does not have to be too detailed, and you should just focus on the main points that will help develop the story.

Keep it simple

It is important to keep your outline simple. Remember that your outline should not be a cage that will limit your imagination. Rather, it should serve as a guide that will help you come up with a meaningful story. Therefore, keep your outline simple, including only the main and important points that should be in your story.

As a rule, small or minor details should not be placed in an outline, except if they are important to the story. The reason why you do not include everything in your outline is to prevent the outline from limiting you to exercise your imagination as you write your story. Again, an outline should only serve as a guide.

You also do not have to make your outline beautifully worded. Do not forget that the outline is only for your own eyes, so you do not have to spend so much effort in finding the right combination of words. You can save such effort for when you finally write the book. Instead of worrying about the words that you use, focus on the story that you want to tell, as well as the flow of the events and information.

Be flexible

It is worth remembering that an outline only functions as a guide. As such, it is not required for you to always stick to your outline. This is important for you to remember, especially if you suddenly come up with a better idea than the one in your outline while writing the story. This is another reason why you should keep your outline as simple as possible. By keeping it simple and just including the important parts of the story, then you will have more room to exercise your imagination.

It is considered very common for writers to suddenly stray away from their original outline. This is why you should not spend so much time worrying about how your outline is written. After all, it is still just a guide for you; and being the writer, you are free not to follow your outline.

Flexibility is important. Normally, the story only reveals itself fully even to the writer only when you actually pen down the story. This may sometimes come as a surprise, even to the author himself. As you write your book, the more you realize what the story is really all about. Simply put, as you follow your outline, you are also led to discover more about it. Now, from time to time, you may have to change course and take a completely different one than what you have originally outlined. This is normal, but just be sure to take a better path than the previous or current one. Also, if you ever change your course, you may want to stop for a while and reflect on the direction of your new outline.

A normal part of flexibility is to be flexible enough to update your outline. Yes, an outline can undergo so many changes and modifications as you write your book. Take note that you do not need to write new outlines, rather you can just edit your current outline little by little.

A common mistake committed by writers is to change a part in an outline and then allow the new storyline to lead the way without him knowing where it will actually go. Then this happens, then it is as good as writing without an outline. Now, I am not saying that this approach is wrong. Again, there are no hard and fast rules about how to write a book. However, if you are the type who cannot write properly and organize your thoughts without a guide, then what you should do in this case is to update your outline. Yes, updating an outline is something that you should do every time you make even minor changes to your outline. The outline must remain logical and coherent all throughout. This will ensure that your novel or the story itself will also be logical, coherent, and well structured. After all, your very story is just the outline itself, only that it now has more details. For example, if your outline says that Samantha is beautiful, then your story will make descriptions or show certain scenes to show just how beautiful she is. Still, the very essence of the writing can be traced back to your simple outline. Outlining and being flexible go hand in hand. Although there are writers who stick completely to their original outline and do not let anything divert their path (which is not wrong per se), sometimes it is good to be more open and allow changes to take place, especially positive changes.

Have a clear premise

Even before you work on an outline, you should first establish your premise. Ask yourself:

- Who is/are my main character/s in the story?

- Where does the story take place? In what year or time?

- What is the conflict in the story?

- What will be the turning point of my story?

- What message do I want the story to communicate to the readers?

- Who will be the enemies in the story, if any?

Once you have answered all these questions, then it means that you have a good idea of what your story will be. Take note that these are just basic questions. You are free to expound and ask more specific questions. But, these questions will reveal to you the premise of your story or what it is really about. Now, in case you find it hard to answer these simple questions, then it only means that you need to think about your story even more. Do not forget that an outline can only be made if you have a story to tell. Although an outline does not need a complete story, it requires that its essential elements should be present.

When you ask yourself these questions, it is important that you be completely honest with yourself. It is unfortunate that some writers delude themselves and hate saying" I don't know." Take note that this is a normal part of the writing process. The more that you admit to yourself the parts in your story that are still unclear to you, then the more you will understand what your story is really about. After all, the act of writing is still an act of self-discovery. You do not need to have the answers right away. It is normal to accept that you do not know the answers to some questions; the important thing is not to stop to seek for an answer. Of course, to do this, you need to reflect and delve more into your story.

Take a break

Just as you take some breaks to finish writing a book, you should also give yourself time to take a break when you are working on an outline. It is not uncommon for professional writers to spends days just to work on their outline. If you are just starting out to learn how to write and use an outline, then feel free to take as much time as you need. Just do not forget that an outline should make the writing of the book to easier in the long run. Unfortunately, some writers get too caught up writing their outlines that they fail to even start writing the actual book.

You will also be able to think much more clearly and be more creative if you allow your mind to relax. In fact, writers are strongly advised to give themselves a break from time to time even while working on the actual book. It is not uncommon to find writers who go to the beach and spend time on vacation while working on a book. This is because you will be a much more effective writer when you allow yourself to rest. With a fresh and rejuvenated mind, you will be able to use your creative talent more effectively.

Choose and organize your ideas

A book comes from an outline. But, where does an outline come from? Yes − an outline comes from ideas. However, it is worth noting that in the process of writing a book, it is very common to experience being bombarded with lots of ideas. For example, let us take a simple example where you present a protagonist in a story. Let us say that your hero is a man who happens to work in secret service for the government. There are tons of different ideas that you can use to show this. There are also many ways by which the story can go. Does he have super powers? Is he going to die and then resurrect? Or is he just an ordinary person who just happens to be good at what he does or maybe he is not even good at his job and merely relies on luck. The thing is that although outlining is a way to record and organize your ideas, you should also choose the ideas that you will be using in your story.

Now, once you have organized the ideas in your mind, it will then be easy for you to plot your story by making an outline. It is simply hard to make an outline when you know that you yourself do not know your story.

Observe proper sequence

When you write your way outline, it is important for you to pay attention to the proper sequence of the events or information. If it is a fiction book, I then the building and arrangement of the story should be in proper order. If you are writing a non-fiction book, then the information should be in an ordered sequence that will make the information more understandable to your audience. This is important especially if you are writing about a technical topic. For a fiction book, you should build up the story from beginning up to the end. In case of a non-fiction book, then you should share the information by starting from the basic details, and then continue building your way up to more complicated topics or sub-topics in the book.

Making an outline is the best way to set the proper sequencing of events of your story. Unfortunately, some writers still write the bulk of words only to end up with a confusing storyline. By making an outline, you can easily work on the sequence of the events of your story. In fact, you will be able to view and imagine your story completely, and all that will be left for you to do is to add in the details.

If you ever find yourself having a hard time putting things in the right sequence of ideas or events, then it is usually a sign that you should pause for a while and try to understand what is really going on in your story. Sometimes the logical sequence itself will be the one to guide you as to what to write next.

Focus on the main points

Making an outline is simply making a list of the important points of the book in proper order. You should focus on the main points. For a fiction book, the main points will be the beginning of the story, the rising action, climax, falling action, and the denouement. In the case of a non-fiction book, the main points, of course, would relate to the important details regarding your subject.

It is worth noting that some minor details may also be considered a necessary element in the development of a story. In this case, you can include the said minor details in your outline.

But, what are the main points? How do you know if a certain detail should be considered a main point and be included in your outline or not? Well, it depends. If the detail or information is something that is important in building up the story, then it is to be considered a main point and should be included in your outline. However, if it is something that your book or story can do without, then it is just a minor detail. The important thing about making an outline is to give you a good sense of direction. It has to function as a logical road map of your thoughts even if you forget about your story. After all, it is not uncommon for writers to think of an exciting plot only to have it slip away before they are able to get it written down completely. Whenever this happens, a possible wonderful story is lost to the world.

It does not have to be perfect

An outline does not need to be perfect. Keep in mind that it is just a guide. Hence, there is no need to follow it to the letter. Even if you come up with what you believe to be a perfect outline, know that it is still just an outline. As such, you should not allow yourself to be limited by it.

It is also worth noting that no matter how perfect you think your outline is, there is still a chance that it may be revised or modified. This is true, especially in the case of novels. It is not uncommon for writers to start at something specific only to be taken by the story somewhere more beautiful than they had imagined before writing the book. Does this mean that writing an outline is not important? Of course not. An outline assures that you maintain sense and direction in your story. However, it is worth noting that it considered common for writers to make changes to their outline several times as they write the book. Now, you should be careful when you do this. As a general rule, you should not change your original outline. You must stick to it. However, as an exception, you may change your outline if you are able to come up with a better version of the story. It has to make the story more exciting or meaningful for the readers. If not, then you need to stick to your outline. This is the reason why you should not aim to have a perfect outline because such a thing simply does not exist.

Although you do not expect an outline to be perfect, it does not mean that the outline can just contain every thought that you think would be good for your story. An outline must still be carefully written. How can you expect for your outline to guide you if the ideas do not match up well with one another or if the outline itself fails to follow a logical sequence? Hence, it is important that you work on your outline, but do not aim for perfection. Having the right ideas and correct flow would be enough.

Now, just because an outline does not have to be perfect does not mean that you should not give it as much time as it deserves. The outline, after all, serves as the foundation of your book. Therefore, take as much time as you need when making your outline, which leads us to the next topic: time.

Remember that an outline is just a guide

Although an outline can be regarded as important, do not forget the fact that an outline is still just your guide. Therefore, you are free to stick to it while you write the book or totally abandon it halfway. However, this does not mean that an outline is no longer important. But, you need to understand this so that you will not end up like other writers who get too obsessed with their outline.

Remember to see and use your outline as a guide in writing the book. You are always free to change or revise your outline as many times as you want and in any way that you deem best.

Take your time

When making an outline, you should take as much time as you need. Although your outline will not be a part of your book, it is still the foundation of your book. Consider it like a business plan or blueprint of your masterpiece.

Although you can make an outline in as fast as a few minutes, it is not uncommon for professional writers to spend even a week to work on an outline. This is true, especially if you want to create a high-quality book.

You should also learn to organize and manage your time. Unfortunately, there are many writers who commit the mistake of procrastinating. The temptation to procrastinate is something that you should watch out for when you write a book. A good way to avoid procrastination is to set daily objectives. For example, aim to be able to finish 15% of your outline every day. Also, take note that writing an outline is just part of the process. The more important part is for you to write your book, which will take more time and effort than writing an outline.

Have your sources ready

This is true, especially if you work on a non-fiction book. You should have your sources ready. This is because sometimes it is hard to look for your sources during the time of actual writing. A good way to keep your outline more organized is to cite your sources in the outline. One of the main reasons for using an outline is to make the work of writing the book easier for you.

You do not have to cite your sources formally. After all, the outline is your own private document. You do not need to show it to your readers or anyone else. The purpose of having your sources ready and to cite your sources is for you to be ready when you write your book. So that when you write the book, you will know exactly where to look for information as you fill in every major and minor topic in your outline. Even fiction writers can use the same approach. After all, many fiction stories also incorporate real-life events. Take, for example, *Da Vinci Code*, which combines fiction with non-fiction information.

When it comes to writing non-fiction, it is important to take note that you should stick to the facts. If you want to force your creative thought and ideas into the page, then you might want to consider shifting to fiction writing. It is worth noting that readers of non-fiction books read not mainly for entertainment or pleasure, but to get as much as useful information as possible. They do not care about your opinions unless your views have a good basis and foundation. Hence, it is important to identify the kind of genre that you want to write in even before you make an outline. This is because the style of writing and even the expectation of the readers have certain distinctions between fiction and non-fiction writing. As for the sources, be sure to quote from credible sources. If possible, use internationally known and accepted formats like APA or Chicago when citing your sources.

Ask yourself questions

Okay, so now you have a clear idea of how to make an outline. But, how do you know which types to include in your outline? The key is to ask yourself questions, the right questions. For example, when writing fiction, let us say that you have a character named Max. Now, ask yourself, who is Max? Let us say that Max is a poet.

Ask yourself who is Max as a poet? What is he like? Once you are able to answer this then you can have something to place in your outline: Max is a poet who writes for a princess who does not even know that he loves her. Next, ask yourself what happens next. You may come up with the next part of the outline, like: A big event is about to take place and Max and the princess are going to attend the said event. The next step is for you to imagine the event and ask yourself what happens to Max at the event, and so on and so forth. As you can see, by simply asking yourself the right questions, you can develop a story.

How about for non-fiction writing? Well, a similar technique can be used. However, if you are dealing with a technical topic, let us say a book about Blockchain technology, then you should ask a different kind of questions. For example: What is blockchain? What are the types of blockchain? What is the history of blockchain? This continues until you come up with a highly informative book.

It is important to ensure that every part of your outline should help develop or enhance the book. This way you can be sure that your book will be interesting and informative.

Okay, so how do you know the right questions to ask? It is simple. You just have to take the perspective of a reader who does not know your book or subject. Therefore, if it is fiction writing or when you write a novel, if you have a character in mind named Gabriel, then ask: Who is Gabriel? What does he do? Where does he live? All these questions will soon open up a whole new story that is full of meaning and value. Now, in the case of non-fiction writing, again just consider that a reader is a beginner in the subject that you are discussing. Therefore, you should start with the basic details and lay down a good foundation. After which, you can then talk about more complicated topics within your subject matter.

Practice

When it comes to learning how to outline properly and more effectively, nothing beats practice. So, if you want to learn how to make an outline, then just start practicing it. Make an outline for the next books that you write. No matter how much you read about it, it remains true that the only way for you to appreciate and realize just how beneficial making an outline can be.

Learning how to write a good outline is just like learning to write good books. This means that you simply have to practice it by applying it regularly. If you get good at writing outlines, then the task of writing a book becomes simpler and more manageable.

You do not have to learn the different ways to outline a book. After all, when you make an outline, you only need to use one method. If you want, you can combine two methods at once. There is no strict rule as to when a particular method should be used over another. Therefore, feel free to use the one that you are most comfortable with.

For those writers who are against the use of an outline:

Indeed, there are some writers who do not like the idea of using an outline. It is worth noting that this book does not make it a requirement or an obligation of a writer to use an outline, but merely shares how helpful an outline can be in the process of writing a book. Therefore, if you strongly prefer not to use an outline, then you are free to do so. In the world of book writing, whether or not you use an outline does not matter in the end. What matters is the final product, which is the book itself. There are writers who use an outline and know for sure how useful it is, while there are those who simply allow the story to unfold like a surprise. The only disadvantage of not having an outline is that it is common to follow a story only to meet a dead end or you just realize that the story has become dull and boring.

An outline assures that before you even start working and writing your boo, you are assured of a good sense of direction. All you need to do is write, and even if all that you do is to stick to your outline and not change any parts of the story but merely add in the details pursuant to your outline, then you can be sure that you will end up with a good book, provided that you have prepared a good outline.

Once again, it is up to you as a writer whether or not to use an outline. The best way to find out what works for you would be to give it a try. Write a book without an outline and then write one that has a proper outline, and see which writing experience is better for you. In the end, it is not about whether or not you have used an outline, but how much the book has made your soul grow in the process.

Conclusion

Thanks for making it through to the end of this book. We hope it was informative and able to provide you with all of the tools you need to achieve your goals whatever they may be.

The next step is to apply everything that you have learned and start making an outline of your book. Learning how to make an outline is one of the best things that should be in the arsenal of every writer. It is useful and makes the book writing process easy and manageable.

If you are a beginner, you might encounter some difficulties writing an outline for the first time. The key is to not be too strict about it. It is worth noting that the methods revealed in this book are also just guides. You, as the writer, has all the right to make your own modifications. In fact, you may want to develop your own way of making an outline. The important thing is for you to know and understand how to use it to help you in writing a book. Keep in mind that there is really no right and wrong way of making an outline as long as it is able to help you write your book. After all, the very purpose of an outline is to help a writer and make the process of writing a book simpler, easier, and more organized.

When you write a book, it is not uncommon to suddenly feel so lost. Some writers have a story to tell but do not know how to start or how to maintain a smooth flow of the pages. This is why making an outline is important. There is a big universe out there, and you need to place only the right stuff into your book in proper order. Indeed, the task of a writer is not an easy thing. But, if you learn how to use an outline, then you have an invaluable weapon that you can use to make the writing process so much easier.

Good luck!